T0170895

BELONGING

BELONGING

poems

DICK DAVIS

Swallow Press / Ohio University Press

Athens

Swallow Press / Ohio University Press, Athens, Ohio 45701
© 2002 by Dick Davis
Printed in the United States of America
All rights reserved
Swallow Press / Ohio University Press books
are printed on acid-free paper ⊗ ™

10 09 08 07 06 05 04 03   5 4 3 2

Library of Congress Cataloging-in-Publication Data
Davis, Dick, 1945–
   Belonging : poems / Dick Davis.
      p. cm.
   ISBN 0-8040-1042-0 (alk. paper) — ISBN 0-8040-1043-9 (pbk. : alk. paper)
   I. Title.

PR6054.A8916 B45 2002
821'.914—dc21

                              2002017749

Acknowledgments

Some of the poems in this book have appeared in *Hudson Review* ("Iran Twenty Years
Ago," "Shadows," "Night Thoughts," "Haydn and Hokusai," "A Monorhyme for the
Shower," "Farewell to the Mentors," "Live Happily," "Out of Time," "To the Persian
Poets"), *Dark Horse* ("Gongora," "Victorian"), *Formalist* ("What"), *Hellas* ("Dido"),
Sewanee Theological Review ("Political Asylum"), *Tundra* ("Checking Out While
Checking In"), *New Criterion* ("Guides for the Soul"), *Threepenny Review* ("Aubade"),
Yale Review ("A Petrarchan Sonnet," "A Se Stesso"), *Profile, Full Face* ("Hiberna-
tion"), and *Critical Quarterly* ("Teresia Sherley"). "In the Restaurant" and "Desire"
appeared in the online journal *failbetter*.

"West South West" was commissioned by the BBC, as part of its celebration of
National Poetry Day, and broadcast on October 5, 2000.

"A Monorhyme for the Shower" appeared as a broadside published by the Aralia
Press, in June 2001.

To the memory of Edgar Bowers

Contents

BELONGING

Shadows

The sun comes up, and soon
The night's thin fall of snow
Fades from the grass as if
It could not wait to go.

But look, a lank line lingers
Beyond the lawn's one tree,
Safe in its shadow still,
Held momentarily.

Delighted my daughter runs
Twisting from my embrace
To touch the fragile snow
Before it leaves no trace.

A Monorhyme for the Shower

Lifting her arms to soap her hair
Her pretty breasts respond—and there
The movement of that buoyant pair
Is like a spell to make me swear
Twenty-odd years have turned to air;
Now she's the girl I didn't dare
Approach, ask out, much less declare
My love to, mired in young despair.

Childbearing, rows, domestic care—
All the prosaic wear and tear
That constitute the life we share—
Slip from her beautiful and bare
Bright body as, made half aware
Of my quick surreptitious stare,
She wrings the water from her hair
And turning smiles to see me there.

Haydn and Hokusai

Masters of wit and line
Who welcome what is ugly,
Lumpish, disproportionate,
And give it grace, distinction—
Whose humor is a pool
For all of us to splash in
(And we emerge like angels
Double-dipped in Pactolus
To shimmer in bright air
That is and is not earthly . . .)

Haydn and Hokusai,
Who say to Anguish, "Go!
Out! *Retro me Satanas!*"
Though you, and more than most,
Have seen its rodent eyes
Burn in the icy dark,
And felt the fetid blast
Of dragon breath assail
Your heart, hearing the slaver
Of wide hyena jaws—

Haydn and Hokusai
Be with me now, lighten
My lumpen moods, drive off
Ungainly panics, spleen,

Purge me of selfish torpor;
Remind me that you loved
Life's dailiness, its quirks
And frumpish joy; and that
If there is heaven on earth
It's here, it's here, it's here.

Night Thoughts

For some, and maybe the majority,
    I know reality
Means what preoccupies their waking hours—
    But not for me

For whom the real is not light's rapid rush
    Of chance and change, day's crush
Of difficulties, duties, deals, distractions—
    But the still hush

Of darkness where my grateful mind has grown
    One with the monotone
Of whispered breath beside me where you sleep
    Embraced, alone.

Iran Twenty Years Ago

Each summer, working there, I'd set off for
The fabled cities—Esfahan, Kashan,
Or Ecbatana, where Hephaestion died;
The poets' towns, Shiraz and Nayshapour;
Or sites now hardly more than villages
Lapped by the desert, Na'in or Ardestan . . .

Their names now mean a dusty back street somewhere
Empty and silent in the vivid sunlight,
A narrow way between the high mud walls—
The worn wood of the doors recessed in them
A talisman to conjure and withhold
The life and lives I never touched or knew.
Sometimes I'd hear a voice, a radio,
But mostly there was silence and my shadow
Until a turn would bring me back to people,
Thoroughfares, and shops . . .

                        Why is it this that stays,
Those empty afternoons that never led
To anything but seemed their own reward
And are more vivid in my memory
Than mosques, bazaars, companionship, and all
The myriad details of an eight-year sojourn;
As if that no epiphany, precisely,
Were the epiphany? As Hafez has it,

To know, you must have gone along that way;
I know they changed my life forever but
I know too that I could not tell myself—
Much less another—what it was I saw,
Or learnt, or brought back from those aimless hours.

To the Persian Poets

For Sarah Johnston

What rights have I, trespassing in your rooms,
Pilfering your lines, sifting your sacred dust,
Searching for what you were and are not now?
As if I came to where Achilles flickered,
Drawn by the blood Odysseus spilt for him.

But, in another tongue, a stranger speaks,
The revenant who shows me what I am;
In whose hermetic words I recognize
The animals and angels of my heart,
My happiness, my longing, my despair.

Political Asylum

My closest friends were killed. I have a life
That's comfortable in almost every way.
I haven't got a job yet, but my wife
Has found a good position with good pay—

Enough to keep us going anyway.
I don't go out much but, you see, my wife
Is out for almost all of every day.
I read a lot and reassess my life.

I've tried to write, but what is there to say?
My friends were killed and this is now my life;
It's almost certain this is where we'll stay.
We like it here, especially my wife.

In History

In history there never was a land
With no one there before we entered it—
Neither God's promises nor *Lebensraum*
Lay listless for the taking: so we carved
On others' faces our predestined map,
And when the voice of God receded, blood
Was on our hands and in our eyes forever.

Gongora

(Whose father was an assayer of goods confiscated by the Inquisition)

The new world's gold—searched out, expropriated—
Brought home in squat, potbellied caravels;
Pain clung to it, pure, unobliterated,
And found new halls of anguish, older hells:
Reworked as filigree and massy plate,
Sword-hilt, menorah, monstrance, crucifix,
Prized objects of virtù, rich gifts of state
Bright with the promise of apocalypse.
A child pokes through them in a lumber room
(His silent father's writing at a table):
Worship and fantasy, and puissant Spain;
Imagined glory gores the velvet gloom.
Violence and glamour tell their lying fable
To one who has no notion now of pain.

A Petrarchan Sonnet

*For David Caplan, who told me that the Marquis de Sade
was a descendant of Petrarch's Laura.*

Here's a coincidence to give one pause:
The poet's perfect paradigm of grace,
Laura's unreachable, dissolving face,
Proleptically, with no overt applause,
Becomes the ultimate, unconscious cause
Of lust's eponymously saddest case—
A prison cell's a fine and private place
For Onan's simple, solipsistic laws.

Justine joins Laura's shade in Paradise
And punishment's the price of *Liberté*,
Not only Petrarch burns in fire and ice,
Not only Laura looks and looks away:
Self-murdered in their dreams of sacrifice
Marquis and Poet shudder and obey.

Casanova

Con man *extraordinaire*, grand cabbalist
Whose angels spell out Leporello's list,

Antaeus who draws strength from touching hearts,
And better-guarded, more lubricious parts;

Shapeshifter, trickster, miracle-producer,
Braw bobby-dazzler, all-the-world seducer,

Commoner, snob, suave crony at the palace,
Ruled only by your own unruly phallus . . .

High on the Doge's roof you slip, flail, crawl—
But our appalled applause won't let you fall.

Dido

"Remember me, but ah! forget my fate . . . "

Aeneas leaves to found his nation-state
And all that we remember is your fate:

The tinsel's torn, transmogrified desire
Extravagantly feeds the fatal pyre;

Your putti scream, then, smudged with smoke, escape
To publish love rewritten now as rape;

And in the gulf the breeze that fills his sails
Wafts to his ears their penitential wails.

In the Restaurant

A queen in exile, she presides at table,
Her weather-eye on rowdy merriment;
Her rule seems easy, even negligent,
But all the family knows her glance is able
To quell or swell the boisterous friendly Babel
That swirls about her, tamed and turbulent:
A Cybele you'd say, embodiment
Of all that's customary, tribal, stable.

Who, seeing this plump matriarch, could guess
That thirty years ago she'd risked her life
To cross Beirut's bomb-cratered no man's land,
Defying anguished parents, to say "Yes"
And be an unbeliever's outcast wife,
Careless of who'd condemn or understand?

Duchy and Shinks

For Catherine Tufariello and Jeremy Telman

Duchy and Shinks, my father's maiden aunts,
Lived at the seaside and kept house together:
They bicycled in every kind of weather
And looked across the waves to far-off France.
Routine had made their days a stately dance,
A spinsters' *pas de deux*, with every feather
Where it ought to be: no one asked them whether
They liked a life with nothing left to chance.

They showed me photographs of long ago—
Two English roses in a chorus line:
I said, "They're lovely" as I sipped my tea.
They were, too—at the *Folies*, second row,
Or downstage, glittering in a grand design,
With every feather where it ought to be.

West South West

Since I was born in Portsmouth, west south west
Would mean the Solent, then the open sea:
A child let loose on Nelson's *Victory*
I fantasized his last quixotic quest,
Trafalgar's carnage—where he coolly dressed
As gaudily as if he wished to be
The natural target for an enemy,
And willed the bullets to his medaled chest.

Hardly a gesture I could emulate.
My west south west was more a stealthy game
To be elsewhere, escape, rewrite my fate
As one who got away. But all the same
I find I walk the shattered deck and wait
For when the marksmen see me, and take aim.

Teresia Sherley

Waking in the Sussex dewfall with the first light showing through,
Hearing English rustlings, stirrings, as the day begins anew,
Grateful for surprise, survival, for my exiled life with you

As my lawless mind betrays me and I'm neither here nor there,
Neither bride nor wife nor mother, still sublimely unaware
That there was a place called England, that we had a life to share—

So in no place I lie hearing sounds that give me to the past,
Wagons creaking, kitchen clatter—but I know the dawn has passed
And no call from dawn's muezzin told me night had gone at last.

Still I stay here for a moment not consenting quite to wake,
Over Esfahan's green gardens I remember morning break,
Yellow light on pools and plane trees, and the shadows that they make

And the sudden breeze of sunrise, like a nervous lover's hands
Hardly touching, but still touching, as my body understands,
Like a whisper that insists on life's importunate demands

Tugging me to love and pleasure, to what passes as we sleep,
To the roses' quick unfolding, to the moments that won't keep,
To the ruin of a childhood, and the tears that parents weep.

When you begged my hand in marriage and the shah gave his consent
Gossip called me Christian payment or a pretty compliment
But I'd seen you and considered what a marriage with you meant—

Strangeness always my companion, at my side and in my bed,
Unknown syllables exulting in my mouth and in my head
Silences I couldn't fathom, all my faux pas left unsaid,

But what's marriage but a launching of a life to the unknown?
Whether yoked to some poor dervish, or the partner to a throne,
Women's lives stay inextricably dependent and alone:

And the glamour of your difference was rubbed amber to a straw,
As I trembled like a mouse beneath some cat's capricious paw
Barely breathing "Yes" when asked if I approved of what I saw.

If the hazards I accepted were no worse than others choose
Still I feared my life without you if it seemed I might refuse—
All the ways I could be left alone with nothing left to lose,

So I came to you, became your wife and, as you said, your friend,
Ignorant of everything—except my nagging need to spend
All my days within the dream-life I could not allow to end.

Promises proliferate; an alien in a curious land,
Drawn to lives I thought I'd be a part of, love, and understand,
Clutching at what can't be closed on by a fumbling foreign hand—

This I shared with you, my darling, when I saw you lost, unsure
As the conversation chanced on turns you hadn't bargained for,
As Rejection smiled urbanely, and Discretion closed the door,

Left you what you were, a stranger, and you saw—whatever *you* did—
Though the phantom Friendship beckoned, smiled and simpered, she
    eluded
All attempts to hold her: you stayed welcomed, baffled, and excluded.

This we shared in Europe, feted in Vienna, Prague and Spain
As the entertaining envoys of the shah's exotic reign,
While the gaudy greetings withered to politely phrased disdain—

And the Vatican, remember, when beneath St. Peter's dome
We were gawked at as the cicerones' chicest sight in Rome,
Dogged by strangeness till we rested in the place that you call home

Where you looked in vain for childhood that you'd thought could
        never change
And you realized that from now on life at best could rearrange
Vistas lived through, and abandoned, and irrevocably strange.

This we shared then, and we share it, and for this I let my eyes
Open on the pallid half-light that I daily recognize
As the emblem of my exile . . . but the harsh nostalgia dies:

Neither Persian, no, nor English, as I see dawn's light erase
Dearest darkness and its phantoms . . . and I'm ready now to face
All of morning's minor duties, all that's weirdly commonplace.

What

Now that the soul's become
A nervous zero-sum,
Something the cortex's
Pavlovian synapses
Produce by accident—
A blur, a taste, a scent,
That seems to (but does not)
Refer back to a what . . .

What is it that your gaze
Locked on my face conveys?
And whose is the colloquy
Of silent sympathy
I share in seeing you?
What is it makes us two
Indivisibly whole,
Dearest, if not the soul?

A World Dies . . .

A world dies when a person dies; who sees
And savors life as he did who is dead?
No one now lives the myriad privacies
That made the life that ends, now, on this bed.

Sweet Pleasure . . .

Sweet Pleasure, my dear, I haven't forgotten
    The vows you delectably made
To stay with me always, come summer, come winter—
    But it was your sister who stayed:

She winked at me, elbowed me, shoved me aside,
    Then trashed every plan I had laid—
A permanent lodger who calls herself Duty,
    A raucous and boorish old maid.

Hibernation

Now that you've gone, and I can't contact you,
I try to live as curled-up dormice do:

Summer's dissolving sweetnesses sustain
The little limbs and heart and dreaming brain,

And I too live off what I stole and kept
From summer foraging, before I slept.

No Going Back

My mother loves deep voices—
Paul Robeson, Kathleen Ferrier—rich,
            Romantic, with the weight
Of tragedy about their lives,
            Odds overcome, succumbed to;
The sob she hears reverberate
            In every note they sang.

For recreation I put on
            High sexless voices—Emma
Kirkby, or some nameless counter-
            tenor whose life I'm happy
To ignore—kidding myself I cruise
            Their cloudless stratosphere;
Transcendent, bright, no weight, no tears.

Secrets

A family full of secrets, of the kind
Well-meaning folk now call dysfunctional;
We always moved but never left behind
The memories we were not allowed to have.

Anguish and pleading and indifference
We each of us played all the roles in turn;
It seemed eternally to make no difference
But we were wrong since one of us was dead.

I ran away to books, fantastic lands,
To verse, where things add up: I came on Rostam
Floundering in the pit his brother's hands
Had dug, pierced by the stakes I knew I'd sharpened.

Out of Time

I woke with sorrow in my mind
　　For no apparent cause
And could not see why I should be
　　Subject to sorrow's laws;

All day, my life seemed out of time,
　　Nagged by a nameless pain
I could not trace to any place;
　　Still it usurped my brain—

Omnivorous and intimate,
　　Growing insistently
Till by day's end it seemed a friend,
　　A fate, a part of me;

Then in the dusk I recognized
　　The day I fear and know;
Grief had not lied, my brother died
　　On this date, years ago.

Aubade

These are the dawn thoughts of an atheist
Vaguely embarrassed by what looks like grace:
Though colors don't objectively exist,
And have no form, and occupy no space,

So that the carpet's sumptuous dyes must make
Bold arabesques untrue as Santa Claus,
And all Matisse's pigments are a fake
Fobbed off on us by intellectual laws,

Though Esfahan and Fauve cannot survive
The deconstructed physics of our seeing,
Still we consent, and actively connive
In their unreal adjustments to our being.

So the thin rhetoric we use to cope
With being so peculiarly here,
Which cannot but be based on baseless hope
And self-constructed images of fear,

Serves to interpret what we are, although
We hesitate to say that what it says
Refers to anything that we could know
Beyond the mind's perpetual paraphrase.

And sensing that no quiddity remains
Outside the island sorceries of sense
(Queen Circe's simulacra in our brains
That make and unmake all experience)

Still, still we long for Light's communion
To pierce and flood our solitary gloom:
Still I am grateful as the rising sun
Picks out the solid colors of my room.

A Se Stesso

As if sheet lightning struck from empty skies:
Incredulous, afraid, you recognize
The way the world's transformed before your eyes.

You have no right to welcome or refuse
Terror and grace that are not yours to choose,
And what you cannot grasp you cannot lose.

Live in the aura of your luck and bow
Before the brilliance that engulfs you now:
It is not yours to hold, or disavow.

"Live Happily"

"Le pauvre enfant, il ne sait pas vivre."

After a while your mind's a *macédoine*
Of muddled poems, stories, paintings, music,
And pointed admonitions by the dead
Who seemed to know what they were saying meant.

In all this incommodious welter one
Phrase comically recurs for me, the flourish
With which Domenico Scarlatti ended
The dedication of his published work—

"Vivi felice" . . . *"Vivi felice,"*
Which I've not done yet, or seen clearly how
I'd manage to. Time's running out, his bright
Arpeggios remind me . . . running out . . .

Guides for the Soul

Who thickens from the shadows as you die?
Who silences your comprehending cry?

Emblem of all you lost and now inherit,
What psychopomp attends your parting spirit?

The unattainable belovèd who
Usurped your life once, and eluded you?

The worshipped clerisy, your sacred dead
Oracular inside your dreaming head?

They may be there—lost somewhere in the host
Of those who welcome your convulsive ghost.

It is a crowd that parts for you, a throng
Among whom now, forever, you belong—

They are the pleas you had no patience for,
The pathos you brushed off: the waiting shore

Is filled with those you failed. You recognize
The sum of what you are in their blank eyes.

Games

What metaphor is adequate?
What image makes a baggy fit?
>   What trope
>   Might cope?

Floods behind levees rising higher
Smooth as a psychopath's desire,
>   Until
>   They spill?

Termites devouring from within,
Till wall and floor are merely skin
>   And all
>   Will fall?

The grinding of tectonic plates?
What power, when mass on vast mass grates,
>   Could halt
>   Earth's jolt?

Nothing so gross or grand you say.
But now that every (every!) day
>   Confirms
>   That worms

Or fire will feed on you—and soon—
What's the appropriate slow tune?
        The phrase
        Which says

That you, for all your games, for all
You might describe, invoke, recall,
        Or cherish,
        Will perish?

Victorian

Dearest, I'd hoped to hear from you today
But Posty had just one for me—from James
(Dear loyal James, who always has to play
On my side in the family's fun and games):

He says that India's indescribable,
And then describes it. He keeps out of harm's
Way, learning Persian verbs. If you still call,
I must convey to you his "Best Salaams."

I've often wondered if his funny nose
Might sniff us out. He'd shield us for my sake,
Then preach at me in private, I suppose.
I know he thought that Charles was a mistake:

The vulgar sermons grated on his nerves
As now they grate on mine. Can it be true
A woman always gets what she deserves?
Charles is quite sure it's so. As if he knew.

I'm sorry that the last time you were here
The girls distracted me. But Florrie's six
And needs me even more than you, my dear—
I can't keep track of all her impish tricks.

And now my Emily has turned fourteen
She's far too pert for Missy to control—

She's *quite* grown up (you know, dear, what I mean).
Missy's a jewel, but has a servant's soul.

I must go now. I'll try to write more later . . .

Friday. Still nothing from you, dearest love:
I hover round poor Posty like a waiter,
I can't think what he thinks I'm thinking of.

My life's made up of Duty, Hope, and Boredom:
You and dear Charles both think I haven't tried.
It's true I dream about what he'd call "whoredom"
(Sitting, demurely naked, at your side—

Is that so bad?—and far away from here).
Charles is so good, I ought to be content:
But darling, honestly, you've no idea
How stultifying life is since you went.

I know you hate this kind of talk . . . I know . . .
But sometimes I'm afraid you're tired of me.
I'm not like you, I can't just come and go,
Bird-like, in your belovèd Italy . . .

I can't, and yet I must, live on without you.
Send poems, darling. Don't be angry. Please.
I won't, I mustn't, nag at you or doubt you.
Have pity on your lonely friend. Louise.

Partners

We've always been inseparable, it's true,
But don't think that implies I'm fond of you;
I get embarrassed by the things you do—

I feel I can't quite trust you anywhere
And everywhere I go you're always there:
No one could call us an attractive pair.

I think you put my friends off: is it spite
Makes you insist on looking such a fright?
Face up to it, you're not a pretty sight.

And then you have the insolence to claim
That I'm the one who's actually to blame,
That I'm responsible for our shared shame

And if I'd paid attention years ago
And worked with you, and not been so *de haut
En bas*, things would be fine. Well, maybe so;

Whatever, as you'd say, you slob. But I'm
Aware you're contemplating pay-back time,
And punishments appropriate to my crime.

Already I can't sleep too well: vague aches
Won't go away, a doctor's visit takes
Forever and she says, "for both our sakes,"

(Though this well-meant advice is hardly new)
That I should take much better care of you.
You have the upper hand now. As I knew.

Just a Small One, As You Insist

The stuff to soften girls and turn the boys on
In vino veritas—clink—name your poison.

What makes parochial differences concur
In one accessible miasmic blur?

The potentate's potations and the peasant's
Admit both rankless to the genial presence

Where torchlight, moonlight, and the brashest neon
Reveal what can't be said but all agree on—

Kindness, knowledge, solace, our glimpse of glory . . .
Tomorrow though is quite a different story.

Desire

The bored house cat Desire likes novelty
And has to check it out—goes sniffing where
She has no business to, extends a paw
By way of tentative experiment,
Pats, and withdraws, pretends indifference,
Then pounces. Something valuable could be
In pieces soon. Think, Kitty, what it is
That curiosity accomplishes.

Farewell to the Mentors

Old bachelors to whom I've turned
    For comfort in my life,
I find you less than useful now
    I've children and a wife;

And though you're great on *Weltschmerz*, loss,
    Lust, irony, old age,
I draw a blank when looking for
    Advice on teenage rage;

On sibling rivalry and rows
    I can't begin to rate you,
You're silent when it comes to screams
    Of "Dad, I really hate you."

So get you gone, Fitz., Edgar, Wystan,
    And dear old Housman too;
It's clear that at this juncture I
    Need other guides than you.

A Bit of Paternity

To tell your weeping child
"This too will pass, believe
Me, I've been here before"

Is to be one who walks
Communing with himself
Along a wintry shore

And thinks his murmured thoughts
Might calm the crashing waves,
The winds' inhuman roar.

Kipling's Kim, Thirty Years On

There's an accent he can't place,
There's a meaning that he misses,
There's a charming foreign face,
Quick caresses, whispered kisses.

There's a sari out of place,
There's his conscience (that's his Mrs.),
There's a future he can't face
(Money's mumbling, kiddies' kisses).

New at It

"You'd like some candy-floss?"
       What child would say, "No"?
She peers entranced into
       The small volcano

Above which I, self-consciously
       Sixteen, preside.
Six eyes sixteen, then hugs
       Her mother's side.

"Give him your pennies then."
       She counts them, one
By one, into my palm;
       One more; she's done.

I wave off wasps, then pour
       Dyed sugar in
The little crater till
       It starts to spin:

She steps back, but returns
       As filaments
Cobwebby, cloudy, pink,
       Ever more dense

Collect about the cane
    I glibly twirl
Within their sticky web.
    "Who's a good girl?"

I ask, offering the cloud,
    (No one else makes it
More stylishly, I think):
    Gravely she takes it.

Déjà Lu

I read my first book through again,
The poems of my messy twenties:
The stench of misery rose up,
Every last stanza stank of it.

And at the time I thought I'd been
So circumspect, impersonal,
Threading my way through myths and meters . . .
I'd never do that now of course.

Growing Up

What changes is the notion life will change;
It won't cohere at last or come out right,
And no perspective renders where you are
The midst of anything but your disquiet.

Old

When I was young I wondered
How men zigzagged and blundered
Into the bile and rage
That enervate old age.

What nags now at my mind
Is how they keep so kind,
Given the blows they bear,
And justified despair.

Small Talk

At the Reception

Oh look, there's What's-his-name . . . No, that's *my* drink . . .
And he's important these days, isn't he?
The *Times* gave him a good review, I think.
I'm sure he'd love to read my poetry.
You know him, don't you? Can't we go and mingle,
And you could introduce me as your friend?
I'll slip my ring off. There, I'm almost single.
This blouse works pretty well if I just bend
A little forward, no? That's sure to get him.
Well, go on then. Oh, who's that awful blonde?
He'd notice me if only she would let him . . .
I wish that I could wave a magic wand . . .
Hey look, she's gone. Come on . . . Why hi! He*llo*
I'm such a crazy fan of yours, you know.

Checking Out While Checking In

The bored and beautiful receptionist
     Who's sick of being nice to jerks
Gives me her "Welcome-keep-your-distance" smile;
     What gross injustice . . . But it works.

The Business Man's Special

The pretty young bring to the coarsely old
Réchauffé dishes, but the sauce is cold.

Et in Arcadia Ego

(on teaching creative writing in Santa Barbara)

A house was rented for the visitor
    Who came to lecture here for one spring quarter:
In house and class his only duties were
    To feed the hummingbirds with sugared water.

Overheard in Khajuraho

Tier upon teeming tier the friezes rise
Of sculpted couples variously entwined,
And tourists gaze with unbelieving eyes
On yoni, lingam, breast, and plump behind.

I didn't hear her question, but the guide,
Respectfully, and gently as a lamb,
Bends to the blue-rinsed matron at his side
And says, "No, mosques are slightly different, ma'am."

Just So

Despite their highly paid positions
Prince Esterházy's picked musicians
Resented being asked to share
His Schloss stuck miles from anywhere:
Pining for their domestic lives
They brooded on their absent wives
Till Papa Haydn gave the prince
The broadest of patrician hints,
And by his Farewell Symphony
Procured their longed-for liberty.

Just so, eight centuries before,
A hardy central Asian corps
Of cavalry who'd had enough
Of forays, fights, and living rough,
Turned to the poet Rudaki
Whose sweet euphonious eulogy
Of Muliyan (the little stream
That bounded home) broke their lord's dream
Of conquest . . . and returned the band
Abruptly to their native land.

Here is one use for artistry:
The insubstantial filigree
Of singing words or wordless song
Can bring us back where we belong.

Notes

Haydn and Hokusai

The last two lines of the poem are a translation of an inscription in the Red Fort, Delhi, built by the Moghul Emperor Shah Jahan (reigned 1627–58).

Iran Twenty Years Ago

Hafez (1326–1389) is perhaps the greatest of Persian lyric poets. Like his predecessor Saʿdi, and his contemporary the female poet Jahan Khatun, he was a native of Shiraz; the poems of all three often praise the beauty of the town and the sweetness of its life. Nayshapour was the hometown of Omar Khayyam, and of the sufi poet Farid uddin Attar.

Dido

The epigraph is from Nahum Tate's libretto to Henry Purcell's *Dido and Aeneas*.

West South West

This poem was commissioned by BBC Radio's celebration of Britain's National Poetry Day (October 5) 2000. A number of poets were each assigned a point of the compass, on which they were asked to write a sonnet.

The historical and geographical details of this poem will be familiar to British readers. The Solent is a channel about fifteen miles long between the south coast of England and the Isle of Wight. Admiral Lord Nelson destroyed the French fleet at the Battle of Trafalgar (1805); he was mortally wounded during the battle, partly because he insisted on wearing his conspicuous admiral's uniform while on deck. His flagship, the *Victory*, is now in dry dock in Portsmouth harbor, and as a boy I often went around it.

Teresia Sherley

The "thrice admirable and undaunted Lady Teresia, the faithful wife of Sir Robert Sherley" was the daughter of a Circassian at the court of Shah Abbas (reigned 1587–1629) of Persia. She seems to have been more or less a present from the shah to Sir Robert, an English adventurer employed for many years at the Persian court. The marriage was apparently a very happy one, and Teresia accompanied her husband on his travels in Europe, where he acted as the shah's (largely unsuccessful) roving ambassador. For a while they settled in Sussex, at Petworth House; a Van Dyke portrait of Teresia still hangs there.

Esfahan was the capital of Persia during the reign of Shah Abbas. He and his successors made it one of the most beautiful cities in the Middle East, filling it with gardens and splendid public buildings, a number of which still survive. The carpets of Esfahan (mentioned in "Aubade") are some of the most sumptuous the country produces.

Secrets
Rostam is the main hero of the Persian epic, *The Shahnameh*. He is killed by his brother Shaghad, who digs a pit lined with stakes, into which Rostam falls.

A Se Stesso
The phrase means "to himself." It is the title of a poem by Leopardi, in the shadow of which my poem was written.

"Live Happily"
The French epigraph was said by his Alpine guide of the young John Ruskin.

Guides for the Soul
Psychopomp: "A conductor of souls to the place of the dead. In Greek a name applied to Charon; more commonly to Hermes, the Anubis of Egypt, and to Apollo" (*OED*).

New at It
Candy-floss: cotton candy.

Just So
Rudaki was a Persian poet of the tenth century. One of his most beguiling poems begins, "The scent of the stream of Muliyan comes to me continually / The memory of the kindness of my friend comes to me continually." This poem is said to have been written at the request of a disgruntled band of warriors as a way of persuading their commander to return home. The ploy was successful.